ALPHABET COLORING & TRACING

This book belongs to

____

____

____

Copyright © 2020

Disclaimer

SAMPLE PAGES

SAMPLE PAGES

SAMPLE PAGES

Blank Page

A a is for **Animals**

Blank Page

Page left blank in case of bleed through from coloring on the other side. Feel free to use this page for doodling, notes or whatever you wish.)

B b is for Bat

Blank Page

Page left blank in case of bleed through from coloring on the other side. Feel free to use this page for doodling, notes or whatever you wish.)

Cc
is for
Cow

Blank Page

Page left blank in case of bleed through from coloring on the other side. Feel free to use this page for doodling, notes or whatever you wish.)

Dd is for
Dolphin

D D d d d

Blank Page

Page left blank in case of bleed through from coloring on the other side. Feel free to use this page for doodling, notes or whatever you wish.)

Ee is for Egg

Blank Page

Page left blank in case of bleed through from coloring on the other side. Feel free to use this page for doodling, notes or whatever you wish.)

Ff
is for
Fish

Blank Page

Page left blank in case of bleed through from coloring on the other side. Feel free to use this page for doodling, notes or whatever you wish.)

G g
is for
Goat

Blank Page

Page left blank in case of bleed through from coloring on the other side. Feel free to use this page for doodling, notes or whatever you wish.)

Hh
is for
Horse

Blank Page

Page left blank in case of bleed through from coloring on the other side. Feel free to use this page for doodling, notes or whatever you wish.)

Ii is for Ice cream

Blank Page

Page left blank in case of bleed through from coloring on the other side. Feel free to use this page for doodling, notes or whatever you wish.)

Jj
is for
Jaguar

Blank Page

Page left blank in case of bleed through from coloring on the other side. Feel free to use this page for doodling, notes or whatever you wish.)

K k *is for* Kangaroo

Blank Page

Page left blank in case of bleed through from coloring on the other side. Feel free to use this page for doodling, notes or whatever you wish.)

Ll
is for
Llama

Blank Page

Page left blank in case of bleed through from coloring on the other side. Feel free to use this page for doodling, notes or whatever you wish.)

Mm *is for* Mouse

Blank Page

Page left blank in case of bleed through from coloring on the other side. Feel free to use this page for doodling, notes or whatever you wish.)

N n is for Nest

Blank Page

Page left blank in case of bleed through from coloring on the other side. Feel free to use this page for doodling, notes or whatever you wish.)

O is for Orange

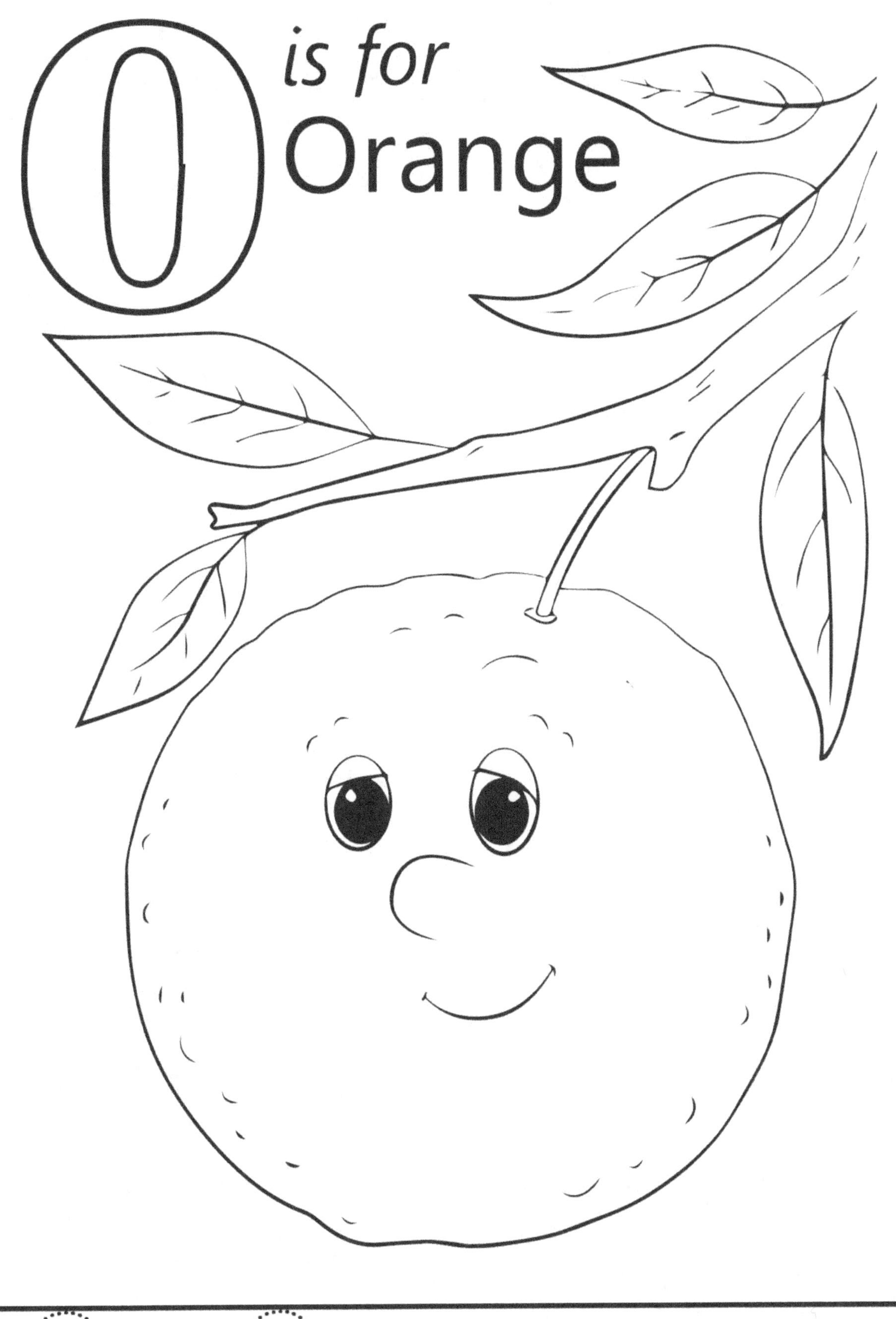

Blank Page

Page left blank in case of bleed through from coloring on the other side. Feel free to use this page for doodling, notes or whatever you wish.)

P p
is for
Parrot

Blank Page

Page left blank in case of bleed through from coloring on the other side. Feel free to use this page for doodling, notes or whatever you wish.)

Q q *is for* Quail

Blank Page

Page left blank in case of bleed through from coloring on the other side. Feel free to use this page for doodling, notes or whatever you wish.)

R r
is for
Rabbit

Blank Page

Page left blank in case of bleed through from coloring on the other side. Feel free to use this page for doodling, notes or whatever you wish.)

S *is for* Spider

Blank Page

Page left blank in case of bleed through from coloring on the other side. Feel free to use this page for doodling, notes or whatever you wish.)

Tt

is for
Turtle 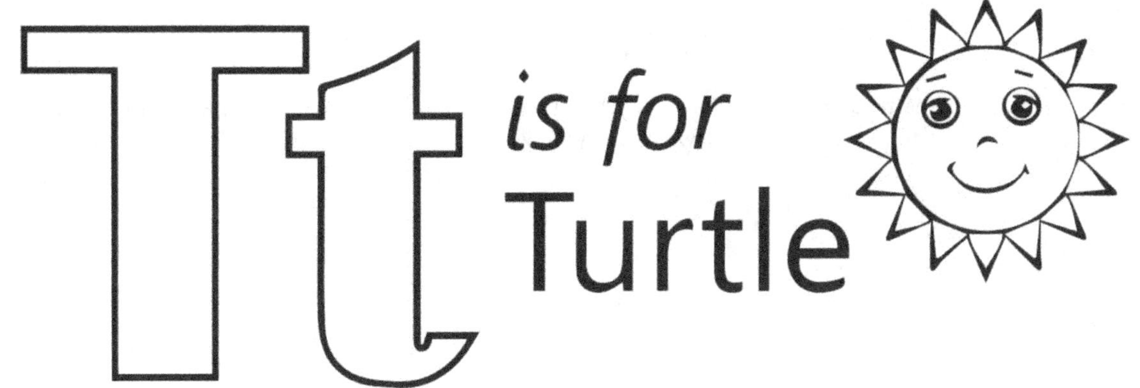

Blank Page

Page left blank in case of bleed through from coloring on the other side. Feel free to use this page for doodling, notes or whatever you wish.)

Uu

is for

Unicorn

Blank Page

Page left blank in case of bleed through from coloring on the other side. Feel free to use this page for doodling, notes or whatever you wish.)

V is for
Vase

Blank Page

Page left blank in case of bleed through from coloring on the other side. Feel free to use this page for doodling, notes or whatever you wish.)

W

is for
Worm

Blank Page

Page left blank in case of bleed through from coloring on the other side. Feel free to use this page for doodling, notes or whatever you wish.)

X is for Xylophone

Blank Page

Page left blank in case of bleed through from coloring on the other side. Feel free to use this page for doodling, notes or whatever you wish.)

Yy is for Yak

Blank Page

Page left blank in case of bleed through from coloring on the other side. Feel free to use this page for doodling, notes or whatever you wish.)

Z is for Zebra

Z *is for*
Zebra